2-45

What a Modern Catholic Believes About

PRIEST-HOOD

by Dennis Geaney and John Ring

 the thomas more press
chicago illinois

WHAT A MODERN CATHOLIC BELIEVES ABOUT PRIESTHOOD

Contents

Chapter One

WHY PRIESTS LEAVE
THE MINISTRY

JUST A FEW SHORT YEARS AGO the priest who left the ministry was rare indeed. If people talked about him at all, it was in whispers; good Catholics wondered what his problem was and they prayed zealously that he might return to the priesthood.

Today the priest who leaves hardly causes a ripple of excitement. We have even passed the time of the dramatic announcement on television or from the pulpit. Now priests just seem to drift away in increasing numbers. Few laymen are shocked; some accept this new phenomenon with relative ease. The majority, however, are confused and distressed to see their priests leave. They do not understand a priest's leaving and they wonder why it has to be.

Young priests speak quite openly now of temporal commitments; some leave within six months of ordination; many leave within the first five years. Those who stay are shaken and distressed by the loss of so many friends. They begin to question their own convictions and the question is always the same: Why do I stay?

Although it may be surprising, it is not only the young priests who are leaving. Many older priests are also leaving the active ministry through early retirement or studied withdrawal. Whereas a few years ago bishops found it difficult to persuade men of sixty-five or seventy to retire, they now find that many priests want to retire at fifty-five or sixty. Exasperated with polarized parish councils, tired of begging to save a seemingly lost school system, and completely unable to understand the new breed of priest and nun, many pastors want out. The tranquility of the retired life has suddenly become very attractive to the harassed pastor. He had always dreamed of having his "own" place. When he finally got it he found that being a pastor no longer carried the same prerogatives. Total acceptance by his assistants, simple reverence on the part of the school sisters, and wide respect by the parishioners are gone. He had expected the life of the pastor to be idyllic; he has discovered it is in fact a painful and difficult life.

What has happened in such a short time? The seminaries are empty, the young priests are dissatisfied, and the older priests are exasperated. The priesthood, once highly esteemed, seems to have fallen on hard times—few want to assume it and many want to abandon it. There are many reasons for priests leaving; it is such a personal decision that there are almost as many reasons as there are priests who have left. Nevertheless, we can include most reasons under the general heading of role conflict, structural breakdown, lack of skills, and personal reasons.

In recent years there has been a growing awareness of the injustices which exist in our society. They weigh heavily upon the American conscience—both on the consciences of those who want to address themselves to these problems and those who want to ignore them. With this increased awareness there has also come the feeling that the Church should somehow be involved in these matters. The Church and churchmen in particular have been called upon to speak out.

However, when the clergy do address themselves to

injustice they find that the adulation on the left is equaled or surpassed by the criticism on the right. What is their role? Few can agree on it; the conflict in society as to their role is matched by the confusion within themselves. What should a priest's role be in these difficult times? It is certain that the tranquil life of the country parson is no more, nor is the Bing Crosby type of priest to be found in our city parishes. Realism has replaced romanticism not only in literature and films but also in real life. The priest who tries to be relevant to the world in which he lives finds out very quickly that he has chosen a difficult role. He no longer commands the esteem of everyone.

Now he finds himself pulled back and forth between those who want him to be a prophet and those who want him to be a priest. This external conflict is matched by an interior one. He would like to be a prophet and "tell it like it is"; he would also like to enjoy the world around him in peace. The new theology has convinced him that the world is good and is ours to enjoy. He does not relish the idea of running against the grain of a world which he now desires and is permitted to enjoy. He has found that the problem with being a prophet is that it is difficult. It is an unpopular role. People may romaticize about the appeal of prophets and prophecy but in the end they still reject the prophet and ignore the prophecy. They don't want to be criticized; they want to be comforted. If you give them a choice between Jeremiah and Melchizedek they will ordinarily choose Melchizedek.

The priest does not know who he should be—Jeremiah or Melchizedek. He would like to be the prophetic Jeremiah but he finds it easier to be the priestly Melchizedek. The young with their intolerance for dishonesty and lack of resoluteness will not accept him if he is not Jeremiah; the older will consider him unfaithful to his priestly vocation and to them if he refuses to be Melchizedek.

What can he do? Which role does he take? Priest or prophet—Melchizedek or Jeremiah. If he becomes Melchizedek he loses the young; if he decides to act as Jeremiah the old reject him. He feels it would be dishonest to act as Jeremiah one day and Melchizedek the next. He does not know how to create a mixture of the two. When he tries to do this he finds himself rejected on both sides. Unable to resolve this dilemma and unwilling to accept continual criticism and rejection, he finally decides that since he can satisfy no one, including himself, he might just as well leave the active ministry.

Years ago there were many structural supports built into the Church for priests. These ranged from a supportive clerical culture to various kinds of organizational incentives. A young man entering the priesthood knew that he was joining the "greatest fraternity in the world." He also knew that he had a definite career ahead of him with several advancements along the way that would culminate the day he would become the pastor of a "good parish" and perhaps even a monsignor. It was all clearly outlined for him—a life of loyal and intimate friends, wide respect throughout society, and personal recongition by the organization. What more could a good organization man want? As for achievements, there were many possibilities. He could build the best plant, the finest school, have the most converts. He had excellent personal support in people and achievements besides belonging to an organization which protected and encouraged him.

What happened? Vatican II broke down the walls separating clergy and laity, thus destroying clerical culture; the priest should not only come from the people but he should remain with the people, and refrain from seeking any kind of organizational advancement. Vatican II informed him that the church must be a sign of hope to the whole world; consequently, he must emphasize quality and not quantity, never measuring his success in terms of numbers. Finally, he was instructed both from above and below that the church is not merely a complex of buildings but the People of God on Pilgrimage and so he should not consider building any lasting monuments.

Clerical culture is something we not only joke about today but we often wonder how we ever tolerated it. Not only do we find the concept of the "greatest fraternity in the world" somewhat ludicrous but we also find it difficult to understand how priests could have lived in an almost exclusively clerical world of golf dates, restricted vacations and private parties—a world apart and to which no layman might belong.

And yet ludicrous as it may have been, a mutual support system was built into the camaraderie of the "greatest fraternity." When we broke down the walls separating the clergy and the laity we also destroyed part of that clerical support system. And rejoice as we might in the greater freedom of movement between clergy and laity, the new faith communities do not yet give the priests the personal support they so desperately need. In destroying clerical culture we destroyed much of their human support. As a result many priests feel that they have been cut adrift and now they are thrashing about to find one or more persons to whom they can anchor their lives. They sometimes find a small community of people to support them. It also happens at times that a sympathetic and understanding woman enters the priest's life at this point and then his notions of celibacy may come into the question. If he is to survive he must have close intimate friends who will support and encourage him.

Horatio Alger—the prototype of success—has long

been a hero for American society. To start at the bottom and end at the top has been a dream and a goal for most Americans. Ours is an achievement oriented society and too often achievement is measured by the salary one commands or the position one holds. It is difficult to challenge this orientation in society; it is impossible not to be affected by it. To live in American society and not feel the need to achieve is a rare thing, a luxury only the young can afford.

The old church was more responsive to this human need than the new church. There was a subtle but very real system of promotions for the priest. He started out as an assistant; eventually became a pastor of a small parish; and then moved from parish to parish, each one a little better than the last until he finally arrived at a "good parish with a good plant and no debt." At this stage he was often awarded the honorary title of monsignor. He had the envy of his peers and the respect of his parishioners. He had arrived. He was someone important. That has all changed.

Not only has the new church stopped making monsignors but with our new sense of the local church the priest is encouraged to dedicate his life to one particular community, thus discouraging him from seeking advancement in the organization. We might add here that this new way of thinking was not imposed on priests. They themselves were the most eager to drop meaningless titles, harmful divisions, and antiquated theology. They were the first to question the old system. Although this may be very popular thinking in our iconoclastic youth culture, secular organizations would be unable to retain their executives with a similar lack of incentives. Abraham Maslow has shown us quite clearly that an organization must meet the ego needs of its members if it is to keep these members. As regards vocation or profession Maslow claims that the organization must meet not only an individual's ego needs but also the needs for self-fulfillment. We want the priest to be human but we tend to forget that he has human needs. The organization today neither gives him the recognition he needs nor does it provide him with many opportunities for self-fulfillment or development. The least happy priests have generally been those in parish work. Those in special work have frequently found sufficient recognition for their achievements and ample opportunities for personal development. The same phenomenon is seen in other areas of American life. The specialist is in; the general practitioner is out. From medicine to academics and throughout the entire professional world, people today feel that they need a specialty if they are going to experience success. The new church has abandoned much of the system which recognized achievement and rewarded it. This may all be very sound theologically but organizationally it is disastrous. It is questionable that such organization will be able to keep its finest young men without the incentive of some kind of organizational recognition.

And even if the organization did not recognize his achievements in the past the priest was able to find satisfaction in other ways. Some men counted the number of baptisms they performed; others counted marriages; there were always some who prided themselves on the number of converts they had made; and there were even some who tallied their confessions and communions. These were all ways in which they could measure their achievements. But now they are being told by the theologians that the church is the *sign* of salvation. The number of baptisms, marriages, converts, confessions, and communions is not important. It is not quantity but quality that matters. Once again no one can quarrel with this theologically but the rest of America does not approach life this way. The small quality company is out; the large conglomerate is in. Society seems to reward quantity not quality. The priest is now asked to concentrate totally on quality. Once again the church is asking him to be out of step with the current trends in society.

Nor is he allowed to express himself through the construction of a fine church or school. He is told that all excess funds should be given to the poor. No monuments please. He is not allowed to take pride in a set of buildings. His works must be interior ones; they must not be seen.

Reading what we've written so far you might possibly conclude that we wish to return to the days of clerical culture—monsignoral rewards and marble monuments. We are not saying that; we are saying that all those phenomena, odious as they may have been, nevertheless had some support value for the priest. In destroying them we also destroyed the support they gave him. If he is to survive in the organization we must develop some new supports for him.

Today the priest is asked to be creative and resourceful and he is asked to be these things with little organizational support. He finds that he is challenged to be someone extraordinary. He cannot hide behind mysteries or miracles. He must stand alone—up against all the currents in society. Although he belongs to an organization which is committed to challenging society he finds that it is woefully inadequate to meet his needs for support and encouragement. He may find some few friends to support him; if he does, then he may succeed. If he must depend on the organization, then he will surely collapse or leave.

It is only recently that the priest has been told that he is to be an agent of change or a catalyst in society. These are new concepts for him and he finds that he does not have the necessary skills to fulfill these functions. Later we will deal at length with the skills necessary for the priest today. We might simply note here that the lack of skills is the cause of much frustration and unhappiness. Many priests consider leaving the priesthood when they begin to feel that they are ineffective. Many do not know what to do; and if they do know *what* to do they do not know *how* to do it.

The world changed on them and the church changed along with it. The successful priest of yesterday frequently finds himself at a loss as to how to minister to people today. He realizes that he is not getting through to them but he does not know what to do about it. His frustration builds to the point where he feels that he must leave. He is very much like the organization man who is edged out of his job because he cannot adjust to new methods. Sometimes he is fired by his boss; more often he decides on his own to leave, frustrated and unhappy.

Many find happiness outside the ministry; others do not. Too many seem to be forced into non-decision-making middle-management positions of American industry. They are not only lost to the active ministry but their opportunities for service to the world are limited. Some become embittered over this; most simply go on to create a new life for themselves. They can be found today in every imaginable occupation in American society.

Role conflict, structural breakdown, and lack of skills could be classified as organizational problems. We have emphasized them because they lead easily to personal problems; they contribute strongly to the growing exodus of priests. It is not so easy to catalogue all the personal difficulties priests encounter today. We will talk about just a few of them.

There seems to be a very dangerous malaise among priests. It is hard to pinpoint or explain but it is very definitely there. There are many reasons for discontent but they are difficult to separate from one another. It has to do with faith, celibacy, the spirit of the times, and many other things. Words such as "tiredness" and "disinterestedness" come to mind. It is difficult to find enthusiastic priests today. Gatherings of priests are often depressing affairs. It is as though they have gone into a funk; they cannot analyze it and they don't know how to get out of it. For many the only way out of the funk is out of the ministry.

For other priests it is a matter of faith. Theologians do not use familiar language today. We may refuse to acknowledge this; we may scratch our heads when the young priests become disturbed in their faith but we have only to read the books of recent years and we will understand how men can become confused. We are discovering many new ways to express our beliefs. The church is in the process of demythologizing itself and things are still up in the air. Since Vatican Council II we have begun to question many facets of the church, things which we previously accepted without question. Today there are few things which we do not question. There are many who cannot yet differentiate between myth and truth. This is true for everyone, not *just* the priest. However, it is more difficult for the priest whose entire life is structured around this faith. When that faith becomes confused, he is bound to become unsteady.

Celibacy may not be the only reason a man leaves the ministry, but the simple fact is that almost all the priests who have left the ministry, eventually have married. It is an issue which will not go away. The rigidity and formalism which once characterized personal relationships for priests are gone. We now live in a highly personalized society. The priest who is unhappy in his work becomes vulnerable. Most priests have deep personal relationships today with both men and women. It is quite natural to turn to a friend for comfort and consolation when in need. Today the unhappy priest will frequently share his feelings openly with his lay friends—something he did not do before. Often the priest is already on his way out of the ministry before he falls in love.

We have left celibacy to the last, for we do feel that there are very definitely other factors which influence a priest to leave and it would not be accurate or honest to ascribe all of a priest's problems to celibacy. However, we do intend to consider the question of the priest's sexuality in the chapter on the *Human Priest*. It is obvious that we cannot say that a priest leaves the ministry exclusively for this or that reason. It is usually because of a mixture of some or all of them. They overlap and intertwine. Some problems can be resolved; some of them cannot. The priest must live with a certain tension in his life. If he is truly to be a man of the world he cannot hope to escape his share of anxiety and discomfort. Nor does it help to have bishops wring their hands and hope that it will all pass away; it will not. If we hope to keep men in the ministry, then the church will have to look carefully at its structures and rebuild them where it can. The priest himself will have to come to terms with a new priesthood in a new society if he is to remain in the ministry.

Chapter Two

THE PRIESTHOOD OF CHRIST

A LARGE SEGMENT of priests who are involved in contemporary problems see that the temper of the times has changed, and that nothing is the same any longer. They are not the same people they were when they entered the seminary. They have become part of the cultural revolution. The personalist approach to life is the very fiber of their being. They see it as a rich expression of the gospel. In St. Paul's language they have put aside servitude and slavery and have become "fed up." The institutional concerns of their anointed leaders turn them off.

During this time the church structures over which the hierarchs preside have given only the appearance of change. In the view of the full-time personnel who are leaving, nothing essential has really changed—this in spite of the kindness and willingness to listen on the part of the elders. Besides being more available, many elders have graciously accepted the changes that have been decreed; in doing this they feel that they have responded adequately. What is frustrating to the moderns is that the elders, for all their good will, seem incapable of responding to the new world. The post conciliar self-studies, renewal committees, weeks and weeks of dialog have made the administrators conversant with the jargon but have not resulted in the great creative personality breakthrough needed to let the gospel ferment in the new cultural leaven. Many feel that they must leave the institutional trappings of Christianity to give Christian witness in the world.

It is not simply the change-oriented people on the cutting edge who are leaving the clerical state. The "bag-packing" phenomenon occurs across the board. If a priest lives in an air-conditioned rectory with color TV, the best kind of food, good laundry service, and no work pressure, could we conceive of his leaving his post? If he finds that all he is doing is perpetuating a folk religion that has little to do with real life, and if he sees people pass the rectory who no longer consider him a vital element in the community, his self image may be damaged and he may entertain the thought that there might be another niche in life that makes more sense to him and to others.

Undoubtedly there is room for delusion, but the hold that the clericalized way of life had on its membership is daily slipping away. Basic to the clerical state is the use of power. In an era in which the clergyman was seen to wield occult powers, to stay the forces of nature, as well as being the gatekeeper for heaven and hell, he had clout at City Hall. "Should I use it?" he often asked himself with great anxiety. Saul Alinsky, a social reformer of this century, successfully pleaded with clergymen to use the power that had been given them as a result of their state of life in order to help people establish their own power blocs in opposition to the entrenched political forces. Many clergy have accepted this notion but with some misgivings. They wanted to identify with the people, but felt uneasy about being pawns in the power brokerage shops. Today, when clergy power is eroding, the priest is losing his magic both with the people and with City Hall.

When he loses his power base in the community, how can he justify his existence? This can present a spiritual crisis in his life. He knows that ordination calls him to servanthood. He understands servanthood as providing services for both soul and body. He may never have grasped the incongruity of the Big Daddy, who always knows what is best for his children, who must also be a servant. Paternalism has been confused with servanthood.

A servant is a man who takes orders and is subject to the will of others who presumably know what is best for themselves. How could a self respecting cleric—bishop, pastor, or associate—switch to a servant role and take orders? How could people who need a father image relate to a priest who rejects the pomp and circumstance of the clerical state and insists on being treated as another man who wants to do their bidding?

The servant model of the New Testament is based on Phil. 2:5ff: "For the divine nature was his from the first; yet he did not think to snatch at equality with God, but made himself nothing assuming the nature of a slave." The cleric by his service retains mastery; the servant model of Jesus Christ sees service as a mutual enterprise. It is something that occurs among people. It is never something done to or even for people.

When we have two styles of ministry built on distinctly different concepts of servanthood and equally divergent needs on the part of the laity we compound institutional confusion. For practical reasons such as cultural lag, a pastor may be forced to accomodate himself to the dependency needs that some of his people have for an authoritarian figure. The point of these remarks is that Vatican II theology has accepted the above kenotic (emptying oneself) model of servanthood and some segments of the church are beginning to carry it to its ministerial conclusion. But when segments of the church are operating at contradictory levels, there is frustration and departures from full time ministry positions. Thus we are led to ask some theological questions about priesthood and ministry—particularly about the priesthood of Christ.

We say that Christ was a priest, but if we look at his life we do not see him in the typical priestly roles of today. He did not live in a rectory, say scheduled masses, wear a clerical uniform, or manage a parish plant. We do see him in a number of other familiar priestly roles. He is concerned with the poor and the afflicted. He rails against the institutional injustices of both church and state. He preaches the kingdom, shapes a discipleship, pledges his continuance after death. He prays, fasts, suffers and dies like every other man. It is difficult to think of him as a priest. He belonged to no priestly caste. In his manner of life he in no way resembled a Jewish priest or the Catholic priests we have known. Does the priesthood we know today evolve from the prophetic life of Jesus who stood up against the establishment? Is the priest in the rectory, whose life is determined by documents from Rome, the chancery office and the expectations of his parishioners that he stay in the sacristy until he is sent for, patterned after the unstructured life of Jesus?

Today theologians and priests are taking a hard look at the Catholic priesthood as we know it and asking themselves if this is the model which Jesus used. There are basically two models which we shall explore in this chapter—the levitical and the pharisaic, or the cultic and the prophetic. These are not mutually exclusive. However, we are asking if the model that Jesus used approximates the one of the Catholic priest of today.

The Catholic priesthood has its roots in both the Jewish tradition of the levitical priesthood and the rabbinate of the Pharisees. The Jewish model for priesthood is contained in the Book of Exodus: "If you obey my voice," says Yahweh to the sons of Israel, "and hold fast to my covenant, you of all the nations shall be my very own. . . . I will count you a kingdom of priests, a consecrated nation."

In this brief passage we see that God, in making a covenant relationship with a people, established a priestly community. Priesthood first of all resides in the people. Although God provided a specific priestly role by assigning the leadership in worship to the tribe of Levi, the priestly people are called, not simply to worship, but to perform the works of justice and mercy.

The Jewish people preferred worship to justice and mercy which is implied in the formation of a community or a covenanted relationship. It seems to be the history of mankind that the religious person would rather say a prayer for a man in trouble than become emotionally involved in helping him. Worship is easier and less costly than responding to human needs.

The message of the scriptures is that God prefers justice to sacrifice. It is dramatically stated in the Book of Micah:

> With what gift shall I come into Yahweh's presence
> and bow down before God on high?
> Shall I come with holocausts,
> with calves one year old?
> What is good has been explained to you, man;
> this is what Yahweh asks of you:
> only this, to act justly,
> to love tenderly
> and to walk humbly with your God.

Although God sent the prophets to remind them of these priorities, they really never heard the message. Cult, or the worship service, dominated the Jewish tradition. They put to death the prophets who tried to tell them to reverse their priorities.

Before Jesus came on the scene there was a reform group called the Pharisees who tried to redress the domination of the levitical priesthood at the expense of the development of the total assembly. The Pharisees have received a bad press because of what Jesus said about them in Matthew's gospel. Today scholars assure us that Jesus was condemning particular abuses of the sect. Actually Christ's model of ministry was not priestly in the levitical sense, that is, centered around worship, but it was pharisaical in that it was a response to the needs of the people.

The leader among the Pharisees was not a priest, but a rabbi. He did not receive his office by heredity but was a man chosen by the community to be their leader. He was a wiseman rather than a scholar. He gave priority to teaching the scriptures rather than offering sacrifice. He was in the prophetic rather than the cultic tradition.

We continually hear that Jesus was a priest according to the order of Melchizedek. This passage from Hebrews is not an attempt to describe his life in existential terms, but to help the Jewish believers see that his life was within the frame of reference of the devout Jew. His high priestly act at the passover meal of the Last Supper was sacrificial and cultic but not cut from a ritualistic pattern of life. The meal was always seen in the context of his crucifixion, which was not viewed as a religious event, but rather the judicial consequences of a man who interferred with politics. He was called rabbi and referred to as a prophet. He spent his life calling people to the works of justice and mercy rather than to the ritual of sacrifice.

If Christ himself did not project the current model of priesthood, it is interesting to see how it developed in

Catholic history. In the emerging church of the first century the leadership roles were in the state of uneven development. There were apostles, elders, bishops and deacons. They were married people who were not set apart from lay people by a distinctive way of life. The apostle was not basically a cult man. It was his job to preach the Good News and form new churches. The elders governed the local church and chose a member of the community to be the cult leader, whom they called bishop. The deacon, while an assistant to the bishop in helping with the Eucharist, had many services to perform in his own right. The priest emerged as the local representative of the bishop in the outlying areas.

The switch from the rabbinical tradition of Jesus, which emphasized explaining the scriptures and serving the community, to the traditionally Jewish levitical orientation became evident as the Constantinian era began to shape the Western world in the fourth century. After the gospel had been preached and entire tribes had been baptized, the only chore left was to service the people with ritual. It is an extremely interesting facet of religious history to see how the pendulum swings from cult to prophecy and back again. While both are the opposite sides of the religious coin, religion falls into disrepute when the cult role predominates for a long period of time. A ministry that neglects the human and the community dimensions of life loses its self respect and credibility and produces a counter ministry.

Martin Luther challenged the church to face the scandal of an over-populated and under-educated clergy that had fallen into disrepute because they were more concerned with piling up graces through the multiplication of masses than they were with vivifying the faith by opening up the scriptures through teaching and preaching.

There were two opposite reactions to the charge. The Protestants wrote off the ordained priesthood as a sacrament and gave new emphasis to proclaiming the Good News through the unfolding of the scriptures. All baptized Christians were priests. They saw no need for a caste within this priesthood of the faithful.

Catholics over-reacted by re-emphasizing the cultic aspect of the priesthood. The seminary system came into being at that time to offer training to candidates for the priesthood so that they might be respectable men. The seminary set out to make the man holy by setting him apart from people and giving him a basic minimum of theological education. Since the sacramental aspect of the priesthood was at stake, the defenders of the faith over-stressed the cultic role of priesthood at the expense of its prophetic role.

It was not until Vatican II that an attempt was made to redress the imbalance. The Council proposed such elementary items as the homily, prayers of the faithful, song, vernacular, and multiple forms of participation to restore the liturgy and the local community as an instrument of prophecy; but more especially, it fostered the notion of the priest himself as a rabbi who speaks to the world about what he discovers by participating in the local church and by being a citizen of this world.

But Vatican II has yet to be accepted as an existential reality by the majority of bishops who signed the decrees and the priests and lay people have given it little more than lip service. With all the good will in the world older clergy and laity still see the priest's role as the keeper of the keys of the tabernacle, as one who makes Jesus available in the form of bread through the words of consecration.

Without rejecting the cultic aspect of the priesthood

the younger clergy see themselves in many roles other than as mere dispensers of sacraments. If they work in an inner city parish, sacramental work is a minor part of their ministry. Ministry today cannot be equated only with the dispensation of sacraments.

The expectations of parishioners may prove to be the exact opposite of those of the younger clergy. The vast majority of ethnic and blue collar parishioners want their priests to stand with Moses on the mountain top. They want him to remain at a respectful distance and be available for weddings, baptisms, funerals and a traditional mass on Sunday at which he gives a sermon that extolls law and order and anathematizes permissiveness at home, church, school or on the streets. There is still mileage left in the system for clerical Agnewism.

Both pre-Vatican II and post-Vatican II priests have their problems with their concepts of themselves as priests over against the majority of pre-Vatican II parishioners and post-Vatican II people who have opted out or are on the fringe, hanging loose. It is easy for the young priest to write off the theologically anti-deluvian parishioner and for the older priest to shake his finger at the hard core liberal parishioners who remind him that he has lost his touch.

A man who accepts an assignment to be a pastor or associate at a parish should not accept the assignment unless he is willing to accept the mentality of the people there together with whatever concept of the priesthood they may have inherited. It is easy to assume a righteous prophetic stance and let the people know how bogged down they are in the backwaters of Christianity. It is a more difficult chore to love people as they are and minister to them, if one can do so with integrity and at *their* point of contact with the sacred. The sensitive and theologically up-to-date priest will always be torn between the need to proclaim the gospel in all its purity, as offensive as this may be to some parishioners, and the need to meet the same with loving acceptance no matter what they may have developed in their own value system.

Chapter Three

THE HUMAN PRIEST

FOR MANY YEARS we Catholics forgot that Christ had a human nature. We were so intent on preserving his divinity that we forgot his humanity. The priest, called to be another Christ, was consequently expected to be something other than human. Today modern Catholics want him to be human—nothing more but certainly nothing less. They do not want him to be a magic or mystical man nor do they want him to be a powerful father figure. They do want him to be a brother—one who shares their life—one who participates in life much the same as they do. They do not want someone who is set apart; they do not want someone who, by virtue of position or title, is somehow above all the fears and frustrations of ordinary life. More than ever before, people are intensely irritated with priests who cannot appreciate the devastating anxieties of life today. In past ages, the priest who remained aloof from these cares and concerns of daily life may have been a tower of strength to the people because of his uninvolvement; today the same priest is rejected because of his lack of involvement. In a world which is desperately trying to recapture the personal and the human, there is simply no place for the priest who is not willing to accept total membership in the human family.

An interesting phenomenon has been occurring in recent years in American society. Whereas many people may have been turned off by institutionalized religion, there are few who have been turned on by the person of Jesus. From the Salinger books of the fifties to the underground newspapers of the late sixties, Jesus is accepted as someone with whom the beleaguered modern man can identify. Modern youth, running from a system they believe to be inhuman, does not only run to the revolutionary Mao. They also buy up and read *Quotations From Chairman Jesus*. It is the human Jesus who appeals to them. They are attracted by the man who spoke with the children, fed the hungry, comforted the sorrowing. They can understand better than their elders why he would weep so pitifully over the rejection of Jerusalem and they can love him for his momentary wavering in the garden or his cold sweat at the realization that he was about to die. In all this they can see how very human he was—how very much like them he was. And they rejoice in this. "Hey, Mrs. Robinson," they sing, "Jesus loves you more than you will know."

The ordinary man is more interested in the words of Jesus than in the words of the theologians. Theological speculation seems to be encased in words which hang in mid-air. They seem to be abstractions with little relevance or meaning for the flesh and blood realities of the *now* generation. The words of Jesus are another thing. He speaks to us about those realities which matter. When he speaks to us of love and fear, loneliness and rejection, we sense that we are listening to someone who has felt all these human emotions. The ring of authenticity is there. Even though several centuries have passed since the days of the "historic" Jesus, his words leap over cultures and traditions. They are real and as charged with human warmth and feeling as the words of a contemporary poet. We have to ask ourselves why it is that modern man seems to be so attracted to Jesus and yet the priest, called to imitate Jesus, finds less and less acceptance. Could it be that priests are not imitating the real Jesus?

The priest who identifies with the human Jesus is in; the one who attempts to create some special kind of clerical role for himself is out. People are attracted to the Jesus of the gospels; they are not attracted by rigorous ritual and complicated ceremonies no matter how hallowed centuries of tradition might have made them. The priest who roots his life in the gospels is in; the man who stands on ritual is out. Simple human values are more cherished than cultural heritage or accepted religious expression.

It is interesting to note that Jesus spent an enormous amount of time in the streets and relatively little time in the temple. The priest today who concerns himself with "churchy" matters is ignored. The man who identifies with the world and concerns himself with all that concerns his brother is accepted and loved. We hear so often today such things as the priest should come from the people and not be superimposed on them. This is just another way of saying that the priest must come from the human family and must not allow himself to lose his humanity or be separated from that family.

Whenever there is a subculture in society those in the subculture do not participate fully in the predominant culture. Clergymen have allowed themselves to be isolated and set apart from the rest of society. They do not participate fully in the life that goes on all about them. The caricature of the clergyman in this century is a devastating one. He seems to dress, speak and act differently. When he walks into a room the conversation is almost always affected as it is by no other professional man. He seems to live in a world all his own somewhere out there on the fringes of real life—never fully participating. We can think immediately of the party scene in "Laugh-In." Everyone at the party is celebrating, with the exception of the clergyman. He stands to one side in his clerical clothes, sipping tea and mouthing platitudes. He does not dance and he does not sing. He does not laugh and we suspect that he does not cry. He is very formal and rigid, much the same as a robot. Is it any wonder that he is ignored? Can we understand now why it is that the Beatles' Father McKenzie sits alone writing the words of a sermon that no one will hear. They will not hear for he does not speak their language. Why is it that the priest so often finds it difficult to communicate with the other members of the human family? Could it be that in many ways he no longer shares that which they all should have in common—their humanness?

The modern Catholic expects the priest to be less clerical and more human. The priest, becoming more and more conscious of the necessity to do just that if he is to be accepted, thrashes about searching for these qualities that will make him more human. If he dares to be fully human then he must know that he will have to be dedicated, unpretentious, honest, open, and compassionate.

More than ever before, the priest today is expected to be a dedicated man. Gone is the day when he was accepted simply because he was a priest. There was a time when he could play golf every day and still command wide respect because of his priesthood. This is no longer true. The modern Catholic will accept him to the extent that he dedicates himself to others. If he is not a dedicated man then they will consider him a parasite on society. It was once taken for granted that a man would support the parish to which he belonged. This is no longer true. We hear of more and more Catholics who are selective about the priests they support. If their local priest is not zealous in his efforts to serve the people then they simply send their contributions to one who is. They do not feel it is their responsibility to support someone who is not doing his job. This is a growing attitude. It will become more prevalent as parochial loyalties break down. The man who is not dedicated will find that he is also ignored.

The pretentious priest is considered an insufferable bore today. He must be unassuming if he is to be accepted. He cannot stand on position or ceremony. He never again must assume that he is someone special—a man set apart. It is necessary to break all the molds of the clerical caste in order to free the priest so that he might once again join the human family and never again pretend that he is not human. "We're all in this together," people want to say to him, "and the only way to get through it is with one another's support. You are what you are. You're one of us. Don't pretend to be anything else."

The priest who dares to take off his collar soon finds that it is quite pleasant not to have to pretend any longer. He need not be afraid. For every man who accepted him for his position there are ten who will accept him for himself. It is not easy to turn a trend or break a mold. However, he will find that there are many who will help him, the effort will be worthwhile. No longer will he maintain an aura of mystery about himself nor will he stand on privilege. All will participate with him in the life of the church. It will no longer be *his* church or *his* liturgy. He will not demand undue respect for his priesthood. Instead he will find respectful love for himself. In short, he will expect nothing, yet he will be overwhelmed by people's response. He will find that it is not so difficult to make it on his own and it is much more rewarding. The release from the pressures of institutional conformity is indeed rewarding. He will never go back into that bog.

Honesty also is demanded of him. "Credibility gap" is a phrase which has only recently entered into our vocabulary. Who can we believe? ask the young. Can we believe anyone in the establishment? The church and the clergy are included in and usually identified with the establishment. There was a time when the word of the clergyman was accepted as something sacred. He was expected to speak the truth. He was not expected to betray the confidence of the people through lies or hypocritical behavior. But because the institutional church has disappointed many, the clergy are trusted less. The church has not been the moral force in society which it was expected to be. Therefore, the priest cannot hope to be accepted as a man of truth simply because of his priesthood. He must stand on his own two feet. In a world filled with so much sham and dishonesty, the priest is asked to have personal integrity. Some may hate him for his honesty, but they will also respect him for it.

When we say that the priest must be honest, we are not speaking of some kind of simpleton who is incapable of a lie. We do say that his basic approach to life and the gospels must be an honest approach. True honesty is as difficult to define as it is to practice. The man who prides himself on his innocence may well be leading a most dishonest life whereas the courageously honest man may also find that he sometimes compromises himself. The modern prophet is not a superman. He, too, has feet of clay.

Related to honesty is openness. Painful as it may be, the priest is expected to be open today. In his former role as the man set apart he was not expected to be open. People could pour out their hearts to him but he was expected to have no heart of his own. He was the man of strength on whom the people depended. He could not show any weakness. He was not expected to waver or falter in his own resolve. People may not have been too surprised to see him laugh; they would have been severely set back to see him cry. And yet priests did cry—when no one saw them.

That is the tragedy of it all—they cried by themselves; they did not feel they could cry in front of others. Too often they were afraid to be themselves. And so they led a schizophrenic kind of existence—hiding their own feelings and showing to others only what they thought others wanted to see. And because they couldn't be themselves they often appeared as empty automatons with programmed responses for every occasion.

But now people are telling the priest that his past life-style was all wrong. Do not be afraid to show us your feet of clay, they tell him. Do not be afraid to cry in front of us. Yet strange as it may sound, the priest finds it extremely difficult to share his own human emotions. He wants to open up and stand before the people as he really is but the years of training and the centuries of tradition have cast certain molds which are difficult to break. Too often he feels that the strong man does not share his human feelings.

How could we have forgotten that Jesus wept? How could we have forgotten that he wavered? He had a human heart which was often near breaking and he was not afraid to show this to the people. There is something inhuman about the man who cannot cry. The priest who is afraid to show people that he cries, by that very act excludes himself from much of human living. Today he must be willing to give up the expected stereotype image of the priest and show himself to people as a fellow human who can be hurt.

Nor is the priest asked to be open only about himself; he is also asked to be open to others—to accept those who do not agree with him or live their lives as he would want them to do. He must not condemn. When he sets himself up as judge, he removes himself from the human race. He places himself above it all.

It is not simply a question of loving the sinner and hating the sin. Today that approach to people smacks of a kind of a paternalism which is completely unacceptable. It is more a question of accepting people as they are with their virtues and their vices. Each individual is unique. All that an individual says and all that he does contributes to making him what he is. The priest who is open-minded will not dissect him, accepting one part but not another. The priest cannot make him over into the kind of person he prefers. He accepts people as they are without trying to reconstruct them to his or anyone else's image. We live in a chaotic and rapidly changing world of shifting values and customs. No one has pat answers to all the questions anymore and the man who thinks he does will simply not make it in our society.

The qualities of warmth and compassion have always been expected of the priest. This is especially true today. Compassion has always been a counterbalance to cruelty. The technological world in which we presently live is cruel in its coldness and impersonal orientation. Young people are rebelling against impersonalism more than anything else. They refuse to accept the impersonalism of the multiversity and the coldness of the large corporation. They are creating their own culture for they cannot accept the harsh and often meaningless culture of their elders. They seek out others who can understand them. Sometimes they create communes for total living but usually they simply huddle together with others for mutual support in their efforts to lead a human life in the midst of an inhuman world. The worker finds himself similarly trapped. He is on a treadmill which never slackens but continually builds up momentum. He races against greater productivity in the factory and spiraling costs at home. He finds that he has less and less control over his own life. There are too many forces aligned against him. He finds he must conform to a world which he did not make and which he may not like.

As with the student, the worker also looks for warmth and understanding. They both hope to find this warmth in their priests. Less and less do they look to the priest as the answer man; they look to him for understanding. If the priest is one who will stand on ceremony or gives answers from a book, then he is no different from the other automatons which one encounters every day in society. They want a priest to listen to them and then respond to their real needs and not to needs which have been projected onto them. In so many ways people are expressing their need for compassionate priests who honestly care about them. They do not want someone who will step back and judge them; they do not want someone to tell them what to do; they do not want someone who stands on ceremony; they do want someone who will listen to them with care and concern. For that man is the compassionate man and that is the man they look for in their priest today. Too often they look in vain. Too often they find the sophisticated dilettante or the social cynic and so they quickly reject him.

Openness and honesty, warmth and compassion—all very human qualities. A man endowed with such qualities would be very human indeed. The priest who attempts to develop these virtues soon finds that his personal life becomes very complicated and risky. He finds himself more and more involved in others' lives. Many have experienced deep pain and acute confusion in allowing themselves to enter into deep personal relationships. It was not only that they were inexperienced in such relationships; they were also suspicious of them. They were caught between the desire to be fully human and the fear that their celibate state made this impossible.

These past few years, our society has been trying new styles of male-female relationships. They have been difficult experiments for the priest. He finds that celibacy has less and less meaning as society rides the crest of the sexual revolution. He finds himself, perhaps for the first time in his life, confronting his own sexuality and asking himself if it is possible to lead a celibate life and have deep personal relationships.

Too many people are constantly saying to him: "The celibacy law is outdated; priests should be allowed to marry." Their intentions are good but such statements intensify confusion for the priest. What can he do? He is struggling with the need to be completely human and the celibacy requirements of the priesthood. Often he loves his life as a priest. He knows that at the present time he must remain celibate if he wants to remain a priest and so he does not find it helpful when people flippantly dismiss the celibacy requirements.

It makes no sense to be pollyannish about the dilemma. It is a very real problem for the priest today and it will not go away. The young priest finds it more and more difficult to accept his celibacy. He is caught in the middle. The needs of the ministry are such that they demand a deeply human minister; but some deeply human ministers have not yet arrived at the plateau where they find themselves comfortable or at peace with the celibate life. Many priests, conscious of their mission, struggle to continue but the pain they experience is at times too great to bear. Suddenly aware of their own sexuality they begin to wonder if it is possible to continue as celibates. They grow tired of terminating relationships that begin to deepen because they endanger the security of their personal lives. For some, their confusion and personal instability grows. Often a priest's professional competency as a minister is affected by this personal confusion. Then, when their peers tell priests that the celibate state makes no sense today, they wonder if it was worth it at all.

A priest can do one of two things in the face of this dilemma. He can easily turn away from every threatening human relationship. This may seem the safer thing to do. In the process, however, he becomes just a little bit less human with every rejected opportunity. If he decides not to run away then he must know that he is in for deep pain and considerable anxiety. His life will never have that easy security again. Many priests have had the courage to love deeply. The signs of their struggle are there for everyone to see. Because of this some have left the priesthood; others have stayed but have become embittered by a difficult situation.

However, there are those who have become exceptionally fine human beings and powerful priests because of the pain they have experienced. These are hard times for those who refuse to take refuge in clerical culture or textbook responses; but they are also good times. We have to believe that such pain has meaning. The laity can see joy, love and compassion on the face of the priest who has made it through the dark tunnel. They recognize that he is truly the salt of the earth and the light of the world.

So many Catholics have already given up on it all. The only contact they could possibly have with the Church is through the human priest—the open and honest priest, the dedicated man who is concerned for his suffering brother, the man who assumes no exalted position and accepts no prerogatives but simply walks the streets of the secular city searching for his brother. That is the priest who will attract people today—the man who is not afraid to love deeply.

Chapter Four

THE PRIESTHOOD: FUNCTION OR A STATE IN LIFE

OLE EXPECTATIONS strike at the heart of the identity crisis in the priesthood. When a person does not know what those above him, his peers, and those below him expect of him, he has to dig into the past to discover his potential. From this examination of his history, he must build his own model—one that is satisfying to him and viable in a church of varying ideologies, ministries and life styles. What we see around us is a model that has worked for centuries, but which is now grinding to a halt. The question that arises is not whether the priesthood will continue, but what will the model look like in the future and will it say anything to the world.

The first place to look for an answer is in the church's official documents on the priesthood. What, beneath the Vatican rhetoric, are these documents saying the priesthood is about? Encyclicals of the popes of this century on the priesthood and the documents of Vatican II show a development but no important breakthrough. They are theological in approach rather than ministerial. They define the priest as an abstraction. They are more interested in what he is essentially than in who he is existentially. Accordingly, the role of the priest is three-faceted: teacher, sanctifier, and administrator; or rabbi, priest, and pastor. These three aspects of priesthood can be extended in meaning so that they fit every situation which the institution has legitimatized by a prior decision. The Vatican appoints a treasurer and then ordains him a bishop. This causes confusion. He is appointed to secular work which is made to fit into priestly categories. We are reluctant to think of priests who work in chancery offices, working with building plans or insurance forms as doing secular work.

The limiting of all the activities of a priest into the teacher, priest, leader triad is called "sacerdotal reductionism." It is too limited as a model for the priesthood today. Like the just price or the just war theories of the middle ages, sacerdotal reductionism is a brilliant conceptualization that worked well for past centuries. With the advent of the industrial revolution, the medieval just price theory was no longer a basis for resolving our industrial ethical problems. When atomic weapons came into our arsenals, the just war theory became useless.

The Vatican II document on the priesthood was considered inadequate at the time of its publication. Vatican II had considered that other issues required more immediate resolutions than did the status of the priesthood in the church and society. It did little more than restate the earlier classical construct of previous popes. It has taken the five years since Vatican II ended for us to begin to see an urgency to building a theology of priesthood and a concept of ministry that will be more supportive of today's priest.

A priest can shift his stance better if he sees the old models not in the limited perspective of theological terms but in the full-bodied light of real life situations. At the turn of the century in Chicago, Father Maurice Dorney was a prime model. Each urban area had its parochial counterpart; Father Dorney was the pastor of St. Gabriel's,

"Back of the Stockyards." The immigrant looking for a job at the stockyards came to the rectory door. When there was labor trouble the pastor was driven in his carriage and tall hat to meet with the owners of the packing industry. When he decided what was best economically for his flock, he could tell them at the Masses on Sunday how to vote. The size of his funeral is still part of the local folklore. This priest was using his priestly power to give his people economic leverage.

By the forties, in the same city, a group of young priests did not feel that this model had any more mileage left in it. They had moved from the writings of Leo XIII to Pius XI, the pope of Catholic Action. In this model the lay people were the front ranks of the Church. The clergy, from pope to priest, made the decisions for the Church. In reality, they considered themselves the church. Yet the laity were encouraged to read, discuss, and act. The priest was not a member of the lay group. He was present as an animator or a guru. This was a step forward. Once laity were encouraged to read and discuss they would soon demand full status in decision making. In the Cardijn, or Pius XI model, the priest kept to the clerical caste but within that framework he tried to help the laity to relate to the spiritual life of each other as members of a family, factory workers, or citizens.

Vatican II, while re-affirming the old priestly model, really opened the door for a new approach to priesthood. Maybe there are many high ranking prelates, priests, and laity who are unaware of it, but Vatican II shifted the roles of priest and laity. Today, the basic unit of the church is the local community. The ordained priest plays just one of the many roles in the community. He is no longer above the community. Although he presides over the liturgy, he is not necessarily the prophetic voice of the community. He may be the animator or sign of unity in the community, but he is not necessarily the wise man. He blends into the community in a way that encourages the community of individual members to reach their full Christian adult potential.

In this view he no longer speaks for the church of the local community. The local community through consensus must speak for itself. This should be a freeing experience for a priest. No longer does he have to see himself as the strong man who must hold the community together by the power of his personality. This may not be a reality yet, but it is the right approach. An indication of the new status of the priest is the inability to tie him to a single role or a simple formula. He may simply be a guru, or he may be an activist on the political scene if he feels that this is his charisma. In an extreme instance, the priest, who is not attached to a specific congregation as an appointed leader and is thus a sign of unity and a minister of reconciliation, should be able to exercise his full citizenship and run for office as a political partisan. (The argument that a priest speaks for the church is archaic because he no longer is the church. As Americans must know, for every Groppi or Berrigan there is a racist or hawkish priest.)

We are moving away from the split-level division of clergy and laity. Within the clergy family, there is a widening gap between bishops and priests and in the household of the laity the priest is finding a new home. The episcopal and lay roles are quite clear. The confusion is about where the priest belongs. Is he a mini bishop or a maxi layman?

The role of the bishop has been quite clear since the second century. He is the successor of the apostles and the focus around which the local churches or assemblies of an area cluster. His principle roles are rabbi, priest, and pastor. If the priest sees himself as a mini bishop, as one who is only a rabbi, priest, and pastor by delegation and nothing else, he may nowadays have serious human problems to cope with. Increasingly we are looking at the priest as a layman who has been ordained but continues to live a basically lay life. He is essentially dedicated to the world and within that context does the works of priestly ministry.

It seems that we are coming back to the role relationships of the early church. It is clericalism and the development of a hierarchical superstructure that has complicated things. Since the clerical state has no basis in scripture, it is quite easy to adjust to a new perspective. It is a product of the Constantinian era in which bishops and priests were lumped into a special caste comparable in status and privilege to the earthly princes. Beyond the court and cloister were the peasants. Clerics could receive the privileges of the hierarchy in return for pledging to be the bishop's faithful servant or identured vassal. The church royalty or clerical state in our times translates into a clerical boarding house called a rectory, clerical clothes, clerical vacations, clerical companions, and praying a monastic breviary. Celibacy is the cement that holds clericalism together.

The question at the bottom of this discussion is whether the priesthood is simply a function or is it a state in life. If it is not a state in life, then the clerical apparatus falls apart and we must deal with the priest as a professional man. If the priesthood *is* a state in life that swallows up a man's humanity and embraces every moment of his waking life, then we must wrap him in the clerical mantle and show him off to the world as a sacred person.

A policeman is a functionary. He does a job, takes off his uniform, and goes home. In his neighborhood he may be a half dozen other things besides husband and father. He may be the head of the Little League, President of the

P.T.A., a moonlighter at the hardware store, and a lector in his parish church. Everyone in the neighborhood knows him as a man whose chief occupation is a policeman, but no one expects that he extend his policeman role beyond working hours unless there is an emergency—at which time they expect him to respond generously and with expertise. No one expects him to live according to a policeman's handbook for how to live off duty. His private life as a policeman may be very public in the neighborhood. He may be the life of the party and wear the loudest clothes when he is off duty without causing anyone to raise an eyebrow. His vocation is seen as a function or a service to the community, not a state in life.

The debate brings into focus the question of the sacred. What makes a person, place, or thing sacred? Today we have trouble with split-level living, putting the sacred and the secular in separate compartments. Today we are searching for the presence of the divine in the world of relationships. We hear the search in the tenement halls of the "Sounds of Silence." Students look for it in rock festivals and Eastern mysticism. Business executives and upper middle class wives seek it in encounter groups. The divine is found in the depths of the human if we search deeply enough. No longer will mankind see the divine simply in persons, places, and things that they are told are sacred. The holy man will be the man who can be recognized as a holy man by his deeds among men. His holiness will illuminate his eyes. Peace and love that have come not from drugs, but from his successful struggle with the demons within him and in the community will give his face a radiance and warmth such that when people's passions subside they will say: "He has made it as a human being. The light of God's countenance shines through him and about him."

An American Catholic touring Europe sees that the sacred places he had heard about in his childhood are now museums. People pour through them everyday behind tourist guides. Indeed they were sacred places centuries ago. They were projections of the faith of the people of a particular era. And it was the people worshipping there that made them holy. The bishop's blessing or consecration of a building confirmed what God had already worked in the people who prayed in this place. Objects or places are holy when people use them as means to reach God. When an object ceases to perform this function, it ceases to be holy.

Ordination does not make a man holy. It is an official call to share in the work of the apostles, to be an official witness of the Catholic church in the world to the gospel of Jesus Christ. Holiness is the result of a *kenosis,* a purging of self that is the result of years of emotional peaks and valleys, fulfillment and despair, agony and ecstasy. Holiness is hastened by prayer—that intimate part of our daily struggles to emerge from the nitty-gritty mess we create for ourselves. It comes from staying in when we are angry, depressed, and generally out of sorts. It comes from accepting rejection. It comes finally from accepting the good that we ourselves and others often find in us. Holiness does not come automatically from offering Mass, conferring sacraments, and reading the psalms. It comes from assuming responsibility for the lives of people and from accomplishing the tasks that emerge from the ensuing relationships.

In our manual of theology we were taught that the sacraments were sacred things. Now we see them as meetings or encounters with Christ. The sacredness of the event depends on our willingness to open ourselves—to kenosis —to what is implied in the ritual action. These words about finding sacredness in the person, the place, or the event are not an attempt to demythologize the sacred but to help locate it more realistically.

When we refuse to reduce the life of a priest to those overt actions which are teaching, cultic and leading, we can begin to see the priesthood in the setting of the local Christian community as it addresses itself to the world. The average priest, then, spends only a limited time in the old pastoral framework. For some priests it is the hour or two he spends in offering Mass at a parish church on Sunday. During the rest of the week he may be employed as a high school or college teacher or administrator. Over half of religious order priests have a job other than pastoral care in a parish setting. Over one-fourth of diocesan priests are likewise so employed.

We have always accepted the priest-scholar, teacher and administrator as well as chancery clerks and financiers as part of the priesthood. Any job a priest had, which came under the jurisdiction of the hierarchy, we considered priestly—sometimes this included janitorial work and driving a school bus. Today we are more willing to look at the work a priest does during the day and identify what is secular and what is ministerial. If one has no hangup about a priest doing secular work, a priest need not apologize for working for full pay for the First National Bank or for a cleric's salary as diocesan treasurer.

The function versus the state-in-life debate came into focus when the time came to set a statutory retirement age for pastors. In large dioceses of the United States the pastor continued to hold his title long after he was unable to say Mass but still able to sign his name to checks. The argument against retirement was that he was a priest forever and taking the pastorate away from him would be taking his real life away from him. Today this hurdle has been jumped. A pastor is beginning to see his ministry as a function rather than as a state in life. He knows that it will end at a certain prescribed time or even earlier if he is not able to cope with change.

Ordination can be seen as a rite which qualifies a candidate for ministry. It makes it possible for the ordained to be called by the local congregation or assigned to a specific ministry by the central agency. If he should be recalled by the local congregation, the higher authorities, or should withdraw for personal reasons he has not lost his priesthood but his call to a particular congregation. The separation of ministry from the priesthood as a state in life seems to be the most revolutionary change in the priesthood in the past decade.

Chapter Five

THE PRIEST—A PROFESSIONAL MAN

THE PRIEST TODAY has been demythologized. No longer do men and boys tip their hats as he passes; no longer do children greet him in a foreign tongue with "Jesus Christ is praised." His celibate existence shrouded in clerical garb no longer gives him any special claim to reverence. If he does not say something through the actions of his life, he is seen as a museum piece or a parasite on the local community.

When we begin to understand the priest not as a sacred person but as one who has functions to perform in society, a new set of criteria emerges. We begin to look at the priest as a professional. It seems to us that any self-respecting priest would want to see himself as a professional man, that is, as a man who has something to offer to the community, something which is tangible enough to be appreciated and for which he can receive the human gratification of knowing that he has done something worthwhile.

For some, the term "professional" has pejorative overtones. It suggests a mercenary getting paid for services which should be performed out of love. It suggests a person who is interested in only one aspect of another person's life. Many prefer the "Big Daddy" action of a priest who dispenses favors from his abundance rather than the concept of a professional priest who has technical competence.

In earlier decades, for instance, members of the St. Vincent de Paul Society looked down upon social workers. The Vincentians saw themselves as men who, after a hard day's work, visited the poor in their homes. They did not see how the professional training of the social worker could match their dedication. One suspects that many volunteers who have no training or supervision may be using others to fulfill their own needs without knowing the harm they might be doing. It is a part of professional training to recognize one's own dependency needs and to separate them from the helping relationship.

It must be understood that when we talk of a professional priesthood or ministry we are not talking about a stifling bureaucracy or about limiting availability or spontaneity. We are saying that a person functions best when he has skills that have been tested and are found to be suitable for the job. The criteria for job description and testing have been developed by his peers out of their tradition. A prospective minister, then, is accountable to himself, to his peers and to the community.

One of the basic securities which a person requires is approval as a performer. This is also the incentive one needs to improve his performance. Without some sign of approval a man can never know if he is doing well, can never feel that he has made it in his career choice; he must suffer the frustrations of doing only what he thinks is best for him to be doing. The thought of an eternal reward is not adequate motivation to improve one's performance. No longer is it sufficient to say a morning offering to insure one's good intentions or an act of contrition to supply for failures that one cannot recognize.

Just a few short years before the decade of the sixties

closed, phenomenal beginnings were made in the professionalization of the Catholic priesthood in the United States. In Chicago a band of diocesan priests determined that they should make a beginning in developing their own standards of performance as well as the conditions under which they would function. They believed that the right to address themselves to these issues, without prior consultation with their bishop, was a step away from slavery or prolonged adolescence and a step toward the development of their manhood. In a short period of time, priests' associations and priests' senates sprang up across the country; these in turn became member groups of the National Federation of Priests' Councils.

The second significant development in the thrust toward the professionalization of the priesthood was the inauguration of diocesan personnel boards. Many bishops showed increased willingness to turn over to a board the power to appoint associate pastors—and in many cases all the appointments—retaining for themselves only a veto power. This meant that priests were to be profiled and consulted by peers. At long last the unique human needs of each priest were considered before a new assignment was made. Associate pastors were no longer to be considered replaceable parts in the ecclesiastical machinery. But such personnel boards are still in the process of learning the skills required for effective personnel management.

It is within the realm of possibility that in this decade we will have a classified ad section or a personnel bulletin which will list job openings for priests who can perform particular functions and for priests who might like to change employment from one part of the diocese to another, or from one part of the country to another. When a priest has the opportunity to draft a resumé, seek interviews, and draw up a contract with defined responsibilities, he will have a built-in incentive to measure up to his own estimation of himself.

The third thrust towards professionalism is the inauguration of the retirement policy and pension funding. In the very designation of this direction, priests are moving from the "womb-to-tomb-paternalism" of the bishop (and the perpetual childhood which it implied) to an adulthood wherein men can have control over the way they live the golden years of their lives. For a body of priests to vote their own retirement by setting up a terminal age means that they maturely place the needs of the people above their own personal security.

A fourth move toward professionalism is for the priests' association to have a say in the determination of financial income. Without any threats, bishops and priests in committee have negotiated reasonable salary adjustments, which in some cases have included a cost of living factor. In some dioceses the centuries old stipend system was wiped out as a source of income in favor of a larger salary. However, these were clerical decisions. Since lay people pay the bills, they must increasingly be represented in future decisions.

Every profession needs prescribed ways of handling grievances among peers as well as grievances with those above and below one in the chain of command. The priests in Washington, D.C., who were penalized for their statement in response to *Humanae Vitae* have kept alive the need for due process for priests. As a result, elaborate machinery drafted by church lawyers is now available in an increasing number of dioceses.

Most of the items we have dealt with thus far are what we call "bread-and-butter" or housekeeping issues. Some think that because a man is a priest he should be so highly motivated that he would be above economic and job security concerns. In actuality, it is unreal to think that we can deal with standards of ministerial performance before we can deal with a man's material security.

How do we set up standards for ministerial performance? The most productive way would seem to be to avoid any theoretic construction of what a priest is essentially and concentrate instead on what he does existentially. The rhetoric of the first-mass sermon or of the silver jubilee describes the priest as the man who spends his life at the altar, in the pulpit, in the confessional, in the counselling parlor, and at the bedside of the dying—a man on call around the clock. But the sacramental priest is no longer the model for the younger clergy.

The fact is that there is presently no single model for the activities of a priest—nor has there ever been only one, nor will there ever be just one. Most priests today wear at least two hats. They are engaged in full time or part time secular work and they also do pastoral work within the structure of the church. The priest who teaches in a high school for two hours a week has a part time secular job even though he may be assigned to it by his bishop. If he takes his teaching assignment seriously he will identify with his fellow teachers as a professional and try constantly to improve his teaching performance. However, in this chapter we are concerned with his professional life as a minister within the institutional church.

High priority must be given to a priest's ability to celebrate liturgy. Prior to the past decade, all that was required of a seminarian was that he learn the rubrics. Military precision and legal exactness were demanded. Today the celebration of the liturgy is an art form. And so, retraining, both intellectual and aesthetical, is required. Most important, a humanization of the celebrant is demanded. A professional association of priests should establish criteria for liturgical performance and offer workshops—either local or national—for retraining.

Every minister of the gospel is at times called upon to be a counselor. One may argue that this function may cease to be a pastoral requirement when a society offers this service adequately through secular agencies. The fact is that pastoral counseling is one of the services that is currently expected of a pastor.

For two decades now, local colleges and universities have been offering counseling courses and workshops at hours convenient for ministers. Today seminaries are amplifying their courses in pastoral counseling and sending their students to Clinical Pastoral Education centers where real life counseling situations are supervised by professionals. A professional association could sponsor similar clinics. Standards would be set up, proficiency would be assessed, and individual priests characterized as more or less proficient in various areas of pastoral counseling. Those innately or temperamentally unqualified in one or another area of counseling would routinely refer clients seeking assistance to others more adept than they. Those whose training did not include counseling skills should be given the opportunity for retraining.

What can be done for the pastor who was trained to keep his distance from people, to deal with them politely and efficiently but cautioned never to expose his humanity to his parishioners? Are there such things as human growth laboratories? As threatening and as explosive as the answer might be to uptight priests, the answer is yes. National Training Laboratories, which is a branch of the N.E.A. has developed such laboratories, and now has almost a quarter century backlog of experience. Since N.T.L.'s inception, the Episcopal Church in the United States has used it for retraining pastors so that they can respond more humanly in individual and group pastoral situations.

A person can find out how he shows his concern to others in the feedback sessions of the human growth labs. This is one approach to learning the art of loving. We are of the belief that loving is a skill or an art that can be acquired in the same way that other skills are acquired. How does one learn judo, boxing, skiing, dancing or any other skill? The location is not a typical classroom. The laboratory is a place where the skill itself can be practiced. The coach or the instructor takes the action apart. He tells the person what to do and then asks him to do it while he watches. After the movement, they dialogue about the action. They examine the experience. It is tried again and re-examined. The parts of the skill are put together and finally the learner passes to that stage when he knows enough to learn on his own without an instructor watching and commenting on his every movement. Human behavior can be dealt with in a similar fashion.

The preacher learns to talk facilely about love, but he may be a cripple in his performance. The mention of the word love bothers many people. Love in the gospel sense means respect, care, responsibility and understanding for the other. It is the ability to move from our self-centeredness to an acceptance of the other person in all his uniqueness without any desire to change the person, but simply to affirm his personhood.

Today a pastor must work with a staff which may include associate pastors, week-end supply priests, sisters, and full time lay assistants. If the staff is to function successfully as a team, the members must share their ideas, their successes and their frustrations with the team and with the parishioners; the pastor must feel secure in this new relationship if he is to work successfully with the team. While the staff or team may be his greatest test, he must face the demand that he work with parish boards, school boards, finance committees and executive boards of church societies. Increasingly he will be forced to use the democratic process, to ask for an early retirement, a rural outpost, or a small ethnic enclave where there is a cultural time lag sufficient to keep him in his authoritarian driver's seat until the statutory age for his retirement.

Management of conflict is a new pastoral skill needed to deal with many of our polarized congregations. Today conflict is viewed as a growth-producing opportunity for both the individual and the community if the leaders have the skills required to keep all sides focused on the issue until it can be resolved. A pastor who can deal with creative tension in his congregation has the unique charism for leading an entire congregation to a new level of spirituality previously unattainable by individual counseling or prophetic preaching. The pastor can acquire these skills at a number of centers across the country which come under the category of Action Training Centers. These centers are linked with both community organizations and schools of theological education.

Many people want to know if the role of community organizer fits the pastoral image. Again, we fall back on our existential approach to priestly roles. Instead of working out of a definition, we ask "what are the pastoral circumstances?"

In recent years the bulldozer has become a familiar sight in the older neighborhoods of our large American cities. Conscious of the fact that many of our cities are showing their age and lack of care, both government officials and citizens have demanded that these areas be razed. Too often urban renewal has caused severe hardship for the poor. The shabbiness of the area may be the subject of conversation in the air-conditioned cars that whiz by on the adjacent expressways, but the poor see their homes as their source of identity and stability. Their simple wisdom tells them that their neighborhoods enshrine precious American and Christian values. As they attempt to push back the bulldozer they look to their priests for leadership and support. They ask that their priest stand shoulder to shoulder with them in their confrontation with "the Man."

Some priests have taken to this work of community organization with great ease and enthusiasm; others have found that they have no stomach for public conflict; still others lack the skills needed for effectiveness. Some priests refuse to enter power struggles of any kind because they feel that they would be in conflict with the gospel. The traps for the priest who enters this work are many. There is the temptation to be a messiah, the danger of imposing a new form of clerical paternalism and the possibility of interfering with the development of grassroots leadership. It takes great wisdom for the minister of the gospel to discern whether his taking the role of community leader is a response to his own personal needs, the needs of the community or both. With these caveats stated, we still defend community organization as a bona fide form of pastoral involvement.

We believe that getting involved in the messy work of helping a community mobilize itself is priestly or pastoral. Unfortunately the word pastoral implies the "shepherd-and-sheep" relationship which does not see the priest as a street worker, a catalytic agent, a facilitator, or one who assumes the role of a civic leader. The fact remains that some neighborhoods will disintegrate if local pastors do not assume civic leadership. To respond by saying that Christ came to save souls, not cities, is not to understand why he wept over the destruction of Jerusalem.

So priests must join other professions in offering continuing education to its membership. No one can consider himself a good practitioner who is not eager to keep abreast of developments in his field. Seminary professors have been making themselves available through institutes and workshops in an effort to update the clergy on new theological insights. Older priests are less threatened by newly-ordained priests and theologically educated lay Catholics and sisters when they are tuned in. It is not necessary that they grasp the new frames of reference, as much as it is helpful if they know that it is legitimate to discuss areas of doctrine on which they had closed the lid tightly. This can be a liberating experience.

While theological education in the sense of exposure to informational lectures helps make a pastor less insecure, it is not what the priest needs most. In fact, this may be a poor method of education. What are most needed are workshops and laboratories in which pastors can deal with faith insight in real situations. Pastors need to learn how one deals with God, Christ, faith, prayer in the lives of people in their natural setting—neighborhood, work or recreation.

This cannot be done with lectures. One of the teaching methods now used in theological education is the case method—what the Menninger Institute calls the "critical incident" and C.P.E. calls the "verbatim" report. People in the field of social work call it process reporting. The pastor can write up an actual case and give his evaluation of his performance and then submit it to fellow pastors to be critiqued by them. In reporting to a group of peers he can learn from them how he might have better handled the case.

Continued education must deal with ethical insights.

No longer do we teach by living up to abstract principles; rather, we may bring to a group the Black Panther, the drug addict, the draft resister and through dialogue with him, under the skillful direction of theologians, the pastor can learn to theologize about public issues.

Professionalism in the priesthood does not demand that every priest be proficient in every pastoral skill. If he is weak in one area, he should seek assistance. In the areas in which he is strong, he should be willing to share his gifts with a wider public. This brings up the subject of "area ministry." With modern transportation, each pastor can serve many parishes with his specialization. Thus he is both a general practitioner and a specialist.

A professional association of priests should establish criteria for ministry that are measurable. A priest's performance should be reviewed by a team periodically. If he fails to meet the minimum standards, the team should make recommendations about how he can improve. If he fails to improve, he would not be recommended for greater responsibility, or he might be asked to take an assignment which is less demanding or to petition for early retirement. A priest has no title to continue in the ministry simply because he is ordained. Skillful performance is the only title a professional has to insure continuing his career. When he has lost the art, justice demands that he not impose himself upon people.

When pastors establish their competency to themselves and to others, it will be reflected in their voices, the carriage of their bodies, and their general feeling of well being. They will demand respect as professional people and thus attract young men to join the ranks of the ministry. It seems to make little sense to appeal to young men to join the ranks of the priesthood if priests themselves are wandering around in a state of confusion as a result of living joyless lives.

The ministry, for those men of faith who believe in the abiding Spirit working in men and who are skilled in the obstetric art of enabling the Spirit to come alive in individuals and groups, will always be the most exciting vocation known to mankind. Ministry for those who are trained and skillful is fulfilling. When one has helped a person grieve, confronted a congregation with their tribalism, or explained the message of Jesus, one has the basis for a rich life. When the ministerial role is clarified there will be laborers in the vineyard.

Chapter Six

THE PRIEST AS PREACHER
OF THE WORD

Everybody's talking at me but I can't hear a word they're saying" is the opening line of a contemporary popular song (from *Midnight Cowboy*). Obviously, it refers to the problems which we all experience in communicating with one another. It could also be appropriately applied to many priests in their efforts to communicate the word of God. Whether preaching in the pulpit, teaching in the classroom, or dialoging in the parlor, they are not getting the message across. People can't hear a word they're saying.

Priests realize that many people turn them off when it is time for the homily at Mass. But no matter how often they realize it and no matter how callous they may have become in the face of criticism, it is always painful to hear. It is painful for they know that man needs to hear the word of God. They also know that it is a primary responsibility of the priest to preach that word.

The priest may have to assume many new roles if he is to function effectively in our society and he may have to adapt some of his old functions to an ever changing scene. However, there are some constants which mark him as a priest; one of these is his role as preacher of the word.

The priest who preaches the word in a vacuum without personally involving himself in the world about him may be completely out of touch with reality, but the priest who never preaches the word because of his involvement in the world's problems is neglecting a primary responsibility. Such secular activities as community organizations, social service, and counseling may be important instruments for social change and personal human development, but so, too, is the gospel of Jesus when properly preached. The priest can and should involve himself in many of these other activities which are both secular and ministerial. However, his dedication to transmitting the good news as such must have a high priority in his life just as it had a high priority in the life of Jesus.

Jesus not only performed great deeds; he also said some very exciting things. People who were personally associated with him were not only affected by his person; they were also affected by what he said. Others who never knew him personally were driven to heroic deeds by the sheer force of his words. It was not that he said something entirely new or different, but somehow he was able to speak to the soul of man. When he spoke of love, for example, and told them how they must love one another, his words were never received as simple platitudes. Somehow he conveyed his own involvement with them. Yet when the priest speaks of love, he is often accused of indulging in empty platitudes. When we preach we don't seem to be able to convey our involvement with the people. They are in doubt as to our personal investment in their lives. Consequently, our sermons often seem to be empty theorizing on general issues. People sometimes become infuriated at a priest's seeming lack of personal involvement. They may begin to wonder: "Is this man human? If not, how can he speak to us of love?" This was never questioned in the case of Jesus. His deep personal involvement with the people animated every word he spoke. He was incapable of empty words.

Jesus could also call people to greatness. When he told them that they were sons of God with a rich heritage, they did not think that his words were empty. They knew that they were sons of God; it was a fact for them, and with the realization of that fact came a growing consciousness of their own immense dignity and worth. Jesus had touched them as no other man had ever touched them before. In the gospels we can see him bringing them the word of God and he does this so clearly that they respond. More than anyone else who lived, Jesus was able to speak to men about God. His presence carried a force and a thrust which mere words are often too brittle to sustain. It was electrifying! People had to stop and listen. In reading the gospels and the Acts of the Apostles we can sense the excitement with which his message was received. Many were so affected that they had to repeat that message to others no matter what the personal cost might be.

Jesus was a master of calling people to personal human growth. It made no difference how humble or unlettered a man might be, in Jesus' eyes he was capable of greatness. Each individual was unique. Jesus was able to touch that uniqueness and call forth that greatness. He brought them a message from their common father and it was a message of great hope. Their father was interested in each and every one of them.

When properly preached, that message has always had an enormous impact on people and consequently on the structures of society. The priest is called upon to preach that same word today, yet we must confess that he is often muted by his own lack of interest or inability to transmit it effectively. He is either too busy about other activities (worthwhile though they may be) or he is unable to translate the word of God into a medium which would be intelligible to the modern world.

It is no mean task to represent God and bring his message to men. It requires not only a knowledge of theology and Sacred Scripture but also a deep insight into the heart of man. If the priest is weak in one of these two areas, he will not be able to speak to men of God. Just as a priest can forget man in his study of theology, so too he can forget God in his study of men. If his theological studies are entirely theoretical, he will never be able to relate what he has learned to men. On the other hand, he could become so involved in activity or the study of human behavior that he neglects to speak of God or his message for man. It is difficult to do both things and consequently we often fail.

This is most unfortunate today for ours is a society which desperately needs to hear God's word. The message of Jesus is a liberating and challenging one. It liberates a man from the fear of his own inadequacies and it challenges him to stand up and proclaim to the whole world that he is quite unique and worthy of respect. The realization of this transforms men. The most ignorant, uncultured and unsophisticated of men can slowly develop a consciousness of his own worth through the study of the gospel message—it is an intensely humanizing process. Such a humanizing process is important today both for the simple peasant of the third world and for the sophisticated scientist of Western civilization. Without the word of God the simple peasant may never know he is a man of great dignity and the scientist may never know he is much less than a god. It is important that they both hear that word.

When we say that the priest must be a capable preacher of the word, we are not talking about the polished speaker or the expert theologian. These things may help a man, but it is also true that the eloquent speaker and the profound theologian are often unable to communicate the message of Jesus; we are speaking of much more. Today's successful preacher is closer to the poet than to the theologian. To preach the word well the priest must be so in touch with his people that he is sensitive to their every need and he is so much a part of his people that he has no difficulty in communicating his love and his concern. He knows instinctively what to say to them, and they recognize him as God's minister and listen to the message he brings them. There are many things which hinder the priest in his attempts to communicate the word of God but two of the principle reasons for his lack of success in this extremely important area of his ministry are his theological training and the institutional life he leads.

Theological training is very often an impediment to preaching the word. We end up preaching theology and not the word—and theological speculation, as necessary as it may be, is not to be identified with the message of Jesus. The missionary generally finds that the native catechist is much more able to communicate the word than he is. The problem of communicating in a foreign language is not his only difficulty, nor can we dismiss it by simply saying the priest could not get down to the level of the people; it is much more than that. Too often he preaches the word in theological terms rather than human terms. Too often he is a prisoner of the theological language that he learned in the seminary. He is unable to break out of that prison into the clear air of human communication.

His theological training taught the priest a language that is foreign to the ears of the people and unfortunately he does not know how to be a theologian without using theological language. It is necessary for the priest today to be able to communicate with the mentality of our time. Whereas poets and contemporary writers have been able to communicate with the soul of man today, the priest is often accused of mouthing platitudes or using unintelligible language. The religious language he uses is not pertinent to the experience of the modern world. Whether he likes it or not, the priest is often considered to be a man from another world using a language foreign to the understanding of the people.

Theological study should help us to understand God's word. It was never intended to substitute for it. Theological terms may be quite familiar to the man who has studied theology and he may be quite comfortable with them. However, they are unintelligible to the ordinary layman. Nor is it only a question of terms; the entire conceptual world of theology is foreign to the man on the street. He neither uses those terms nor thinks in those concepts. The priest must learn to use his theological studies to help him better preach God's word and not to teach theology.

Perhaps the example of the poet or the novelist might help us understand this. The poet today is sensitive to all that is affecting man and therefore he knows how to touch us. He can speak to us of all the important human values because he knows our language. The good poet, for example, can write about the experience of love without ever calling it by name. Although the word may never appear, the feeling of love is present in every word he writes. He can write a beautiful poem full of hope without saying at the beginning, "I am going to write a poem about hope." When Rod McKuen sings, people listen. They understand every word he is saying and they know he is singing from his own experience. If we were to recall all the sermons we have ever heard, we would probably remember that many of them were theological in concept and language. The priest may break down the theological language but he seldom breaks out of the conceptual world of the theologians. Is it any wonder that the young man in love, the harassed mother, or the worried father is not listening?

The inability of priests to communicate is also due to the institutional life they lead. They often employ an unreal language which is incapable of conveying their ideas and their feelings precisely because they have withdrawn from reality. Priests live differently; it is as simple as that. Institutional life whether found in the army, school, prison or the rectory is quite different from the life of the ordinary citizen, and although the soldier or the prisoner may experience frustrations and difficulties of their own, they are not frustrations and difficulties of the man struggling with the twenty-five year mortgage or the rebellious child. So it is with the priest; his institutional form of life has caused him to be out of touch with reality. It protects him from many of the anxieties of modern life. He himself does not have the same kind of experiences as others in society. Consequently, he speaks of religion and not of the reality of religious experience.

Rectory life, for all its drawbacks, is nevertheless a life of privilege and isolation. The rectory is usually the only house in the neighborhood that can boast of a maid and a cook. The priests are the only men in the neighborhood who never have to cut the lawn or take out the garbage. We say that it is good for the priest to have these services for he can then dedicate every minute of his time to his apostolic endeavors. But that argument is much like the celibacy argument. Some say that a priest must be totally free of any human entanglements so that he might better service the people. Unfortunately, in freeing the priest to serve the people, we have frequently isolated him from them. Because of this isolation, many of the ordinary and routine experiences of the people are foreign to the experience of the priest. The rectory is just a little bit different. It is not quite like the other buildings in the neighborhood. The priests who live in the rectory live a little differently. Therefore, they don't know where to shop for the best bargains and they never experience a full day of washing windows or cutting lawns. Consequently, their sermons seldom reflect the ordinary experiences of the people in the pews.

Because of this style of life, priests can be unfamiliar with the ordinary anxieties and frustrations of their people. They may be able to speak eloquently of the big issues such as race and war. Indeed, they should speak of these issues. However, although many people are concerned with such issues, they are more bothered by the cost of living, the security of their employment, the welfare of their families, and the state of their neighborhood. We may quarrel with this state of affairs; we may say this should not be but the fact remains that it is. This is where people are at. It may be the role of the preacher to call them to greatness; he may be the only one who can make them conscious of the larger issues but he will never do it unless he starts where the people are. Too often he does not know where the people are, for his style of life prevents him from sharing their life.

Jesus spoke of very ordinary things. He seldom mentioned the state of the world. His speech is full of terms which were familiar to the people. He could talk knowingly to farmers and to fishermen. He even understood the chores of the housewife (and so he uses the example of the dough and the yeast). He knew his people well for he did not live apart from them. Outside of the forty days he spent in the desert, he was always with someone—either in the home of a friend or on the road with his companions. It could never be said of him that he led an institutional form of life. The priest today must learn to live with the people if he hopes to speak effectively to them. He must not live in isolation.

Because of his theological training and his institutional form of life the priest is a man of another experience, of a religion that was vigorous in the past. He is not in the present. His religious language expresses a type of religious experience fundamentally different from that which is natural to the modern man, and for this reason it is difficult to establish communication with modern man's existence. He cannot preach the Word if he is not integrated with the human reality in which he must preach. If he does not feel within himself the hopes and sufferings of the people, how can he show them the invisible meaning of these realities; how can he point out the reality of salvation which is fulfilled through these? He will not know the language with which to bring the word of God to the hearts of men unless he has first learned that language from them.

Many priests are painfully aware that their lives are out of touch and they are making valiant efforts to change their style of life and learn the language of the modern world. They know that concern for the affairs of the world is necessary if they are to effectively preach the word. Others, in their efforts to become a part of the modern world, forget their mission to preach the word and busy themselves exclusively with secular concerns. They think that the faith will maintain itself or develop new structures in which it can live and grow. Sometimes priests think that this faith will grow and spread, even if the word is not preached. They sometimes think that the faith will continue no matter what. And so they give preaching the word a very low priority.

We are watching the disintegration of the old structures of our faith; many of the ways in which we formerly expressed it are no longer acceptable. This is not only true of our religious language but also of many of our religious rites. However, we cannot think that the disintegration of faith will automatically produce new faith. Personal and active faith results from personal and active conversion, and personal conversion is a response to the word when that word is preached effectively.

How might the minister of the word preach more effectively today? To do that he must fully understand the society in which he lives. He must be a part of it; only then will he know what to say. There will be a natural spontaneity to his words such as occurs when good friends join in conversation. Their words are not forced or artificial. The caricature of the priest in the pulpit is that of a man quite removed from the people in the pews; they let him ramble on. The caricature is obviously extreme but we all recognize it. There is something unreal about the way priests now communicate the word of God.

The man sitting in the pews today is far removed from the man who occupied that same place twenty years ago. Society has changed and man has changed along with it. Much of that which was important twenty years ago is no longer important. Much of that which is important today was unheard of twenty years ago. It is almost as though our urbanized technological society has created a new man; it has certainly created a new language. To successfully preach the word of God today the priest must know that new man and learn his language. Only then will he be an effective preacher.

Chapter Seven

THE SPIRITUAL LIFE
OF TODAY'S PRIEST

A GROUP OF PRIESTS were meeting to discuss prayer in their lives. It took well over an hour for the group to tackle the subject head-on. They were more concerned with the conditions of life which kept them from praying. The largest concern seemed to be where they lived, which somehow had an effect upon their job fulfillment. Let's talk about this before getting to the spiritual side of things.

Should a priest own his own home or rent an apartment away from the parish buildings? The minister who has a parsonage provided for him as a part of his salary might ask the same question. His home, too, is close to his office and does not allow sufficient psychic space between his family life and his work. He has nothing to do with the selection of his living space. He is not making a choice. He is reminded in many ways that the parish is providing the house for him. He can easily feel like a kept man.

Not every priest wants to live outside a rectory. The biggest objections to moving outside are simple service items such as the cleaning of one's room, meals, taking of telephone messages and the chores a married man normally does. Priests seem very interested in fighting for the right to move out of a rectory; but when it comes to moving into an apartment of their choice, they are often reluctant.

There are other factors more subtle than household chores. Living in the rectory of the parish in which one works means living in the house of the pastor who is your boss during your work hours. He is your boss at work and at home. You live in *his* house and you can't forget it no matter how hard he tries to make you feel at home. Since he hires the housekeeper her basic loyalties are with the pastor. This is usually reflected in the menu and in the decline in the quality of service on the pastor's day off.

There are a number of options that could be offered to associate pastors who feel that their masculinity is threatened or that their human development is arrested by living all of their life under one roof. One option would be to give each priest an allowance for board and room. If he chooses to live in the rectory of the parish in which he works, he can pay the pastor and feel that he can register his complaints as any tenant or boarder does when he shells out his hard earned money. What is more demeaning to a man than to ask as a favor what is owed to him in justice?

Another option for a man who feels quite comfortable with rectory living, but who does not like to live with his boss, is to live in another rectory with priests with whom he shares a congenial relationship. There are some people with whom we can work well and others with whom we find it easy to relax. Personnel boards are overburdened trying to find combinations of people who can work and relax together. A priest should not have to negotiate with the board about his choice of living companions.

Still another option for a group of priests in an area, regardless of their occupational titles, is to set up a clerical boarding house for which the group assumes responsibility. There are a number of examples of such experiments. In the discussion mentioned a pastor who does not like rectory life expressed a personal preference for living by himself in an apartment. He did not see cooking as a major problem. He saw living alone as the best of all celibate arrangements. There was a touch of sadness in his humor. But such existential factors cannot be ignored in discussing the spiritual life of the contemporary priest.

The priest has heard many talks, read many books, and had private conferences on the need for fidelity to a spiritual program. In the sixteenth century, the Council of Trent established a seminary that was designed to give the priest, besides an intellectual approach to Christianity, a solid foundation in Christian piety. It wisely wanted pastors to have the experience of prayer in the seminary in the hope that what they experienced in the seminary would become the pattern of their personal lives.

Time somehow has a way of extracting the substance from a rich insight and leaving the shell. Seminary piety had elaborate forms. It began with morning prayers long before most men had stumbled out of bed. There were long periods of silence for prayer, and a quiet Mass which left much opportunity for personal communion with God. There was silence at breakfast, reading at other meals, silence at night, visits to the Blessed Sacrament, devotions to Our Lady, stations, benedictions—each in its proper season. Each seminary had its variations or specialties, but there was a core formula for the seminarian which, it was hoped, would be such a part of him that it would be the warp and woof of the fabric of his priestly life. He should be able to coast through life and slide into heaven by being faithful to these seminary or monastic practices.

The ideal prayer life consisted of praying the breviary (ideally spread through the day in order that each part may be sanctified), daily meditation from fifteen minutes to a half hour (preferably in the morning) and daily Mass.

Night prayers, communal and private, in connection with a visit to the Blessed Sacrament sealed a day not too far removed from the tabernacle. Annual retreats interlarded with monthly days of recollection were used to keep students and priests feeling guilty about missing meditation and other practices. There were always ample opportunities for confession to deal with this guilt and at times have it reinforced.

Where have these four centuries of tradition for piety gone? How could it fade so rapidly in less than a decade? The priests in the discussion group did not want to talk about it. In polling the group about how many were saying the breviary we found only a scattered few were still saying it totally or in part. Since omitting the entire breviary or substantial parts of it for a single day without a proportionately serious reason is classified as a mortal sin, someone asked the group if their not saying it was a matter of confession. No one in the group considered putting the breviary aside to be sinful neglect.

The group did not care to talk about the seminary formula for piety or prayer. It no longer seemed to be a relevant way of reaching God. It could well be that the formula had been an excellent one and parts of it can still have great meaning, but somehow they felt that they had been unfairly indoctrinated into a system that was not totally viable. A system whose formulation was alien to them had been imposed upon them. They saw the present as the time to throw overboard the authoritarian structures that came from the medieval monasteries and to try to find a way of relating to God that could grow out of their life experience.

Life experience is the key to the prayer life of today's priest. He prays best when he is "in there" pastorally with people. When he is sweating out their anxieties, sharing their fears and doubts, he feels drawn to God. When he goes down into the valley of the shadow of death with another human being, he feels his own limitations, his inability to articulate his faith, his helplessness in crises. In these moments he is able to cast his care upon the Lord and prayerfully ask for deliverance. Without a life of pastoral care, the priest may live an arid prayer life. He needs to be on the growing edge of life and feel its uncertainty in order to pray with passion to the God who has called him to this vocation.

Finding God in the grind of pastoral experience was not exactly a discovery as the priests discussed their prayer life. As Bishop Robinson writes in *Honest to God* (Westminster Press, p. 93):

> I can testify to this most strongly from the time I spent in a theological college, both as a student and as a teacher. Here was a laboratory for prayer. Here one ought to be able to pray, if ever one could. For here were all the conditions laid on—time, space, quiet. And here were the teachers, the classics of the spiritual life, and all the aids and manuals. If one failed in these circumstances what hope was there later on—when one was surrounded and sucked down by the "world" . . . . But, if I am honest, what enlightenment I have had on decisions has almost always come not when I have gone away and stood back from them, but precisely as I have *wrestled through* all the most practical pros and cons, usually with other people. And this activity, undertaken by a Christian trusting and expecting that God is there, would seem to be prayer.

This seems to be where prayer is at in the priesthood among men who feel that they are not called to the monastic life but to a life that is a sharing of the untidiness of one's own life with the messiness of another's. The fact is that young priests have a greater yearning for group prayer experience than their up-tight elders.

Our discussion finally moved in this direction. A young priest told how he needs others to pray through difficult situations with him. A seminary professor made the statement (amazing to the elder priests) that informal prayer meetings are now a normal part of the life of their diocesan theological seminary. A student or a professor will simply put a note on the board that he would like to pray with anyone who would care to pray with him at 10:00 or so in the evening.

A young priest in the group, in discussing the prayerful celebration of the Eucharist, spoke against celebrating the Eucharist so frequently that it ceases to be meaningful—the celebrant has no freshness or creativeness to bring to it. No longer is the daily recitation of Mass a compulsion with young priests. It must be a celebration, not in the Saturday night on-the-town sense, but the Eucharist must be an expression of something that has touched their lives in a most profound way. It must say each time that God lives, loves us, and is present in the very specific areas of our lives. The rapid Mass said at a side altar to fulfill an obligation or to earn a stipend makes today's priest cringe.

One of the staples of a spiritual life, regardless of whether it is Christian or Eastern, is that there must be times in life when one can be alone. Every minister of the gospel must find out how to achieve this balance between pre-occupation and identification with another's struggle and his own need for a psychic space in which he can be alone and let his spirit uncoil. It seems best, however, that no formula be offered.

Everyone must discover ways to re-create himself so that he can tune in to the spirit world and thus discover his relationship with the transcendent God. Every minister needs to separate himself not only from those to whom he ministers but also from his family. Some can do it through long walks, playing a piano, listening to an opera, long periods in the chapel, praying the rosary while driving, lying on a beach, swimming, or reading poetry. Each person who struggles with coming closer to the living God will master the art of restoring a passive dimension to an active life without a how-to-do-it manual or taking yoga lessons.

The discussion group listed theologizing on the secular and sacred as a form of prayer. When younger priests meet for a theological discussion they are not looking for information. This can be mailed to them for their reading. They want to wrestle together with the ethical issues of the day. They are not simply asking what is the party line on race, war, birth control, abortion, and Catholic schools. They want to get insights on the existential dimensions of each issue. They want a climate of freedom to pervade a discussion, which means a respect for opinions which differ from the common view.

In facing pastoral or critical ethical problems together, we find that we reveal our true selves. When we unmask ourselves with our peers and let them see us for what we are, there is the possibility of true communion or friendship. In the old clerical clubhouse camaraderie, there is much golfing and good living but little true friendship. At cocktail parties we can clink our glasses, make a great deal of noise, tell stories that get funnier as the drinking continues—but when it's over, we often go home sad and lonely. Friendships grow out of facing life, all of life, together. Ministers who share the agonies of their ministry with other members of the pastoral team (and not simply the priest members) are shaping a prayer community, regardless of whether or not there is formal prayer.

If we had to unify all the elements of this chapter on the modern priest's view of prayer, we would say that he feels that prayer must begin with a sense of each man's worth and an assurance of his identity as a person. His work and the conditions of his life after work, therefore, are essential ingredients in a healthy prayer life.

The priest is not obsessed with fulfilling routine obligations to God by compulsively racing through prayers that make no sense to him. Instead, he wants to search for God and be free to find him where he will. He finds God not simply in the beauties of nature or in works of art but in his own and his people's struggle to make sense out of the pain and suffering that is often sandwiched between those peak periods of joy as we await our moment of death. He is not worrying about fidelity to prayer as much as he is worrying about his fidelity to the demands that the ministry makes upon him. If he is faithful to his fellow man, he knows with quiet confidence that he is being faithful to God. This is his prayer.

Chapter Eight

THE FUTURE OF
THE PRIESTHOOD

SPECULATION about what the church of the future will look like is filled with traps. Social and cultural forces are exploding into new elements so rapidly that we are unable to discern emerging patterns with any kind of certainty. It is in this vortex of cataclysmic change that the church has to seek a new understanding of its mission. Certainly it cannot be programmed.

Many feel that the church in the United States is simply dedicated to maintaining the status quo, that is, trying to keep the lid on structures that have outlived their usefulness. Preservation of past forms in a period of dynamic upheaval can only hasten the day, they feel, when Catholic churches across the country become national museums much like the missions of Father Serra in California.

Some priests, upon leaving the ministry, quite naively see themselves as prophets who by their exodus are hastening the day when the church will be forced to deal realistically with the issues of a new church in a new culture. They seem to think that if enough priests leave, the shortage will become so acute that the pressing questions about the future of the church will have to be asked.

This assumption, however, ignores sociological realities. In recent years about 10% of the clergy have left their posts. This has scarcely inconvenienced the Sunday churchgoer. The facade of the Catholic Church in the United States as it is today can conceivably be maintained for decades without any change.

The authors wish to propose another view which is neither sociological nor political. It is motivated by a belief in the Spirit active in the church today. This Spirit is calling forth members at the grassroots level to live the gospel in the world of men, and summoning them to build out of the remains of crumbling present structures new responses which will more accurately convey their belief in Christ. These signs of the times are present if we are discerning.

There are a number of parishes across the country which are attracting people because of the quality of the service. People are coming to mass not to prevent guilt, but to celebrate the goodness of God and their trust in life. This style of ministry offers hopeful prospects for the future. Any new ministry demands of its priests richly developed human qualities and special skills in the art of celebrating and preaching.

There are communities of Catholics growing outside parish or ecclesiastical structures and they at times find need for an ordained minister to lead them in the Eucharistic celebration. This is a very natural development that defies bureaucratic organization—at least people are trying to manage with a minimum. "Floating parishes," as they are called, attempt to establish community relationships that are more personal and responsive to an individual's needs. The people who are developing such communities have had a taste of vital Christian community perhaps through their participation in the Christian Family Movement, the cursillo or other groups that find satisfaction in sharing and experiencing the gospel. This development hardly seems to require full time priests which means that these groups will undoubtedly raise the question of whether the liturgical leadership could not be assigned to a member of the group.

The priest-scholar, a species of the hyphenated priest, has always been an important Christian witness in our society. There is no reason to think that the future will diminish his importance. A person who is schooled or experienced in a secular science or art and has a profound grasp of theological understanding and Christian insight will always have something to say to the world. If he keeps alive the tension inherent in his dual role, he will be preaching the gospel in a medium that the world can grasp and relate to.

Another hyphenated version is the priest-prophet. He is the priest who is more interested in toppling over the idols with which man surrounds himself than in the pastoral care of person-to-person relationships. However, there is no need for a large number of prophets. Our media of communication are so pervasive that charismatic figures like the late Dr. King or Father Groppi can be heard by virtually every family in the nation on the day they raise their prophetic voices.

Vatican II offered a possibility of breaking through the stereotyped roles of ministry by restoring the permanent diaconate. What will come of the diaconate can only be speculation. If the permanent deacon is to be a mini-priest, a sacramental assistant, the move will be a regressive one. Laymen already can be delegated to be sacramental assistants such as communion distributors.

The permanent deacon, if he is to bring a new and needed dimension to the church and the world, must be a leader in the local community. He must have a constituency, something which the priest may never achieve since he has been sent into the community by an outside agency to offer a universal dimension to a situation which, by its nature, will always be provincial. The deacon, therefore, is not substituting for the vanishing clergyman, but adding a new ingredient to a formula that has been losing its tang.

What will be the duties of the permanent deacon? This is like asking what specific function does each indigenous leader of a local community perform? He does what he as a community leader deems must be done in the here and now. His agenda will change as the needs of the community change. But why train and ordain community leaders? A person can give a special kind of gospel witness when he has been selected by the community. But with special training in the theological implications of Christianity, he can assume responsibility for and give accountability to the local Christian community. We can expect that a man of the world will be more sensitive if he is supported spiritually by the local church.

The permanent diaconate will hopefully force us to think of an indigenous church, a Latin church, a black church, a hard hat church, a suburban church. Each has its witness to bear and a unique message for the other segments of society. Each deacon should represent the interests of his local church and concentrate on its particular view; hopefully each community will become more and more open to the other views of life represented by other churches.

When will we be able to have women priests and deaconesses? J.F.K. was able to set the end of the sixties as the target date for putting a man on the moon. The timetable was predictable because he was dealing with technological progress rather than religious sensibilities. While it may be helpful to examine what has happened in the past few years, it would be futile to make any projections or construct any timetables. The question of whether women could be ordained was raised only a few years ago by Karl Rahner. He answered his own question by saying that there was no scriptural or theological reason forbidding it. The obstacles preventing women from entering our seminaries and becoming ordained priests are simply cultural. The move to ordain women priests is part of the larger struggle of mankind to give women their equal rights.

The Protestant churches which have opened the ordained ministry to women have difficulty placing women as pastors. The difficulty is not with any policy from their respective headquarters, but rather with rank and file parishioners. An attractive, unemployed woman minister remarked to one of the authors: "If I were a pastor of a suburban parish, what woman would permit her husband to have me as his minister?" A male pastor does not seem to be the same sort of threat to husbands fearful of their wives' affections being alienated through a sermon, counseling, or church work. We are dealing with cultural rather than specifically religious values.

While it now seems to be light years from the day when we will be able to casually accept the announcement that our bishop is pregnant again, there is some progress. Catholic women are studying theology at our universities. What may seem like mere tokenisms from the Vatican are significant telltales of movement. Women are permitted to be lectors and distribute Holy Communion. Although the decrees are highly qualified, the principle has been established.

One's views of priesthood and ministry will determine the form of training for these services. In spite of the dwindling enrollment in the present seminary system, the advances in theological education are phenomenal. Many theologates with small enrollments have been closed; others have moved to urban sites on university campuses where they can form "clusters" or alliances with other Catholics, Protestants, and free church schools of theology.

Seminaries are adjusting their educational approach to ministry so that an updated version can serve the church of today and also be able to adapt to the emerging church of the future. Students are no longer content with theory, but want training in the skills they will use as ministers. Increasingly, Catholic schools of theological education are willing to see themselves as schools of ministry. This will not bring an end to the questioning, but rather begin a new series of inquiries of how one prepares for Christian ministry.

It seems that there will emerge two distinct types of theological education. One will be in a university setting where theology will be pursued as an object of inquiry like any other branch of learning. This will be the training ground for professional theologians who may or may not be ordained to the priesthood or diaconate. The graduates will staff the college and university faculties and they will be the faculty members of schools of ministry as well as be advisors to church administrators.

Crystal ball gazing is a heady game and leads to statements which often become a source of embarrassment to the authors. With this caveat, we will present a model of the future centers for training ministers. The center should be located near intersecting expressways or be easily accessible to public transportation. The center would be open all day and evening, including weekends. Its greatest class loads would be in the evenings for people who work during the day, and on weekends for suburbanites and others who cannot arrange a day or evening schedule.

The student body would be comprised of men and women of all ages above twenty-five. It would include married couples, single men and women, priests and religious. It would be open to people preparing for the priesthood and the diaconate, to men and women who have no intention of seeking ordination but who wish to pick up particular ministry skills. It would also be open to priests who wish to prepare for the decades ahead. Obviously, such a training center would offer a large variety of programs wherein each student, with the help of the staff, would be able to tailor his own curriculum to suit his needs. More demanding requirements would be placed on candidates for the priesthood.

The advantage of diverse training programs for various types of ministries located under one roof is based on the premise that training for ministry should be in a laboratory situation. The richer the mix of the student body, the richer the data for education. People, not books, are the data for learning ministerial skills. The presence of women on the staff and in the student body would be essential, apart from whether the ordination of women is ever resolved in our lifetime. Women teach men by their presence.

Ministry deals with the value systems that give meaning to life. This requires that we scuttle the lecture method and learn to deal with our values and the values of the others through dialog. In ministering, a student is going to use the teaching methods he has learned or has been exposed to in his training. The lecture method is fatal for the minister of today.

The group-dialog method demands that the professor be emotionally secure. The group method itself is a ministry tool which the student must acquire. It sets a style for his ministry which non-verbally communicates his belief that people have something to teach him and that the ordinary person has wisdom to share with the group. It is a teaching method that trusts and respects the learner. One of its objects is to free people or inspire confidence in them to become self-learners.

The curriculum would be a response to the cultural expectations of ministry today. For example, many parishes wish to have their liturgical committee help prepare liturgies. A ministry school could offer courses in celebration, wherein the students learn transferrable skills through laboratory situations. A ministry school could offer parish lay committees the skills for resolving conflict and generally explaining how groups function. Courses in church finances could be offered to parish finance committees.

Priests and students for the priesthood and diaconate would have a greater concentration on bible and history. These courses should not be presented as they are in graduate schools. Scripture and theology professors must learn the new methods of teaching and learn to present their material for people who are going to spend more time on the street than they are in libraries. Ministry is a relational art, not an academic skill. This is not an anti-intellectual statement any more than it is to say that a carpenter is not a good tradesman because he has not read a library of books on architecture.

The ability to pray and the ability to love are basic skills for ministry. If the minister is lacking in faith, acquiring new techniques will not assure him of being effective. Likewise if the minister has no natural empathy, counseling courses will not supply it. For these reasons, the screening committee which will admit students will have to be more interested in the natural human qualities and Christian values in the applicants than in the credits they have accumulated, which merely represent schooling rather than wisdom.

In conclusion, we see less need for ordained full time priests in the future, a greater need for deacons who will emerge from the people, and a greater variety of ministries to be performed by both men and women who operate out of a local community, which has great autonomy, but is linked to the larger units of the church.